NATIONAL
GEOGR

READING EXPE

KIDS AROUND THE WORLD

Wayra's Gift

A Story from Peru

By Adrienne Frater
Illustrated by Rick Powell

PICTURE CREDITS

4 Mapping Specialists, Ltd.; 3-7, 45-48 (borders) © Flat Earth/Fotosearch Stock Photography; 5 (top) © John Cleare/Worldwide Picture Library/Alamy; 5 (center) © Arco Images/Alamy; 5 (bottom) © Glen Allison/ Getty Images; 45 © Ric Ergenbright/Corbis; 46 (top) © Angelo Cavalli/Getty Images; 46 (bottom) © Pilar Olivares/Reuters/Corbis; 48 © Ulrike Welsch (inset), © Pablo Corral V/Corbis (background).

PUBLISHED BY THE NATIONAL GEOGRAPHIC SOCIETY

Produced through the worldwide resources of the National Geographic Society, John M. Fahey, Jr., President and Chief Executive Officer; Gilbert M. Grosvenor, Chairman of the Board.

PREPARED BY NATIONAL GEOGRAPHIC SCHOOL PUBLISHING

Sheron Long, Chief Executive Officer; Samuel Gesumaria, President; Francis Downey, Vice President and Publisher; Richard Easby, Editorial Manager; Anne M. Stone, Editor; Margaret Sidlosky, Director of Design and Illustrations; Jim Hiscott, Design Manager; Cynthia Olson, Ruth Ann Thompson, Art Directors; Matt Wascavage, Director of Publishing Services; Lisa Pergolizzi, Production Manager.

MANUFACTURING AND QUALITY CONTROL

Christopher A. Liedel, Chief Financial Officer; Phillip L. Schlosser, Vice President; Clifton M. Brown III, Director.

CONSULTANT

Mary Anne Wengel

BOOK DESIGN

Steve Curtis Design, Inc.

Published by the National Geographic Society
1145 17th Street N.W.
Washington, D.C. 20036-4688

Product #4U1005109
ISBN: 978-1-4263-5102-0

Printed in Mexico.

11 10 09 08 07
10 9 8 7 6 5 4 3 2 1

Contents

Peru

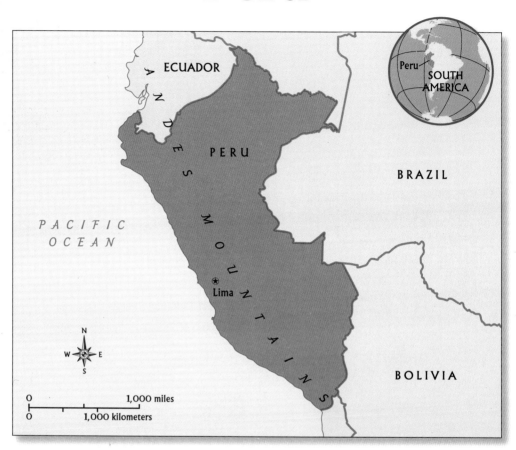

Peru is a country on the west coast of South America. It is about the size of Alaska. Several countries border Peru. These include Ecuador, Brazil and Bolivia. Peru also touches the Pacific Ocean. About 27 million people live in Peru. Many have roots in both native and Spanish cultures. The capital of Peru is Lima.

Geography

Peru has mountains, desert areas, and rainforest. Most people live in the desert or mountains. The Andes Mountains run the length of Peru.

Climate

Peru has several different climates. Along the coast, the weather is mild even though the land is a desert. High in the mountains, the climate is cold and dry. The rainforest is hot and humid with heavy rains.

People

Long ago, native peoples such as the Inca created powerful civilizations. Later, the Spanish entered Peru and brought their own traditions. Today, most people speak Spanish. Quechua is the second most spoken language.

Wayra's Gift

Wayra

Wayra (pronounced WHY-ruh) is a Quechua boy in Peru. He likes to play music on his flute. He also studies local wildlife.

Kusi

Kusi (KOO-see) is Wayra's younger sister. She wants to learn how to weave traditional Quechua designs.

Grandfather

Wayra's grandfather carves flutes to sell at a local market. He thinks Wayra has important things to say.

Father

Wayra's father is a porter on ancient Inca trails. He carries packs for tourists who aren't used to the steep land.

Tony

Tony is a filmmaker from Canada. He is working on a film about the Quechua people.

CHAPTER ONE

Ollantaytambo

Wayra was out of breath. At last he had reached his special place on the mountainside. He climbed onto a large block of stone. He felt the sun's warmth soak into his legs. Way below, he could see his friends playing soccer. They looked as small as ants.

Wayra sighed. He'd like to be playing soccer too. But he'd been born with one leg shorter than the other. His team was practicing for an important match. He knew he was too slow. So each night after school, Wayra climbed up to his special block of stone.

It was one of the blocks the Inca had left behind when they built the Ollantaytambo temple and fortress. That was more than five hundred years ago. The town Wayra lived in was named after these buildings. All the way across the valley he could see the fortress ruins. They towered over the town.

Wayra was proud to live in Ollantaytambo. Tourists came from all over the world to visit his town. It was the only town in Peru where people still kept many of the old Inca ways.

Wayra was Quechua. His family was related to the Inca. Some Quechua still lived in stone houses built five or six hundred years ago. They fetched water from channels built by the Inca. The stone roads still carried Inca names. People still dressed in brightly colored traditional clothes. Wayra liked living in a town where the old ways mixed with the new.

Wayra pulled his flute out of his pocket. He played while he watched his friends in the valley below. His father and grandfather also played the flute. Music was like breathing to Wayra. Last year his grandfather had taught him how to make flutes from bamboo.

Wayra played a tune about the condor. It was a Quechua song. His people had sung it for hundreds of years. Wayra had never seen a condor—but one day he hoped to. The giant bird was special. His people believed it was the messenger of the sacred mountain gods. Weavers wove it into their weavings. Potters painted it on their pots. As he played, Wayra imagined the condor flying from mountaintop to mountaintop. Soon he felt he was flying too.

Wayra put down his flute when he saw his younger sister. Each day before school she walked the alpacas up to their pastures. After school she climbed the mountain again to bring them down. Alpacas and llamas were very important to the Quechua. People used their wool for weaving. The animals also helped carry heavy loads.

"Why did you stop playing?" Kusi asked. "I like to hear your music." She sat next to her brother. The alpacas grazed nearby.

"Ssh," said Wayra. He pointed to a flash of color. "It's that butterfly I told you about." The butterfly was blue. It had a splash of pink on each wing. Wayra could name most butterflies on this part of the mountain.

"I'm worried," Wayra said to his sister. "The government is planning a new highway. It will pass close by our town. We know it will destroy many Inca **terraces.** But it could harm our wildlife as well. The mayor is holding a meeting tonight to talk about it. I'd really like to go."

Kusi nodded. She understood why Wayra was worried. She watched the butterfly fly off, then gave a big yawn. "I'm hungry," she said. "Let's go home."

terrace – a cut made in a hillside to create level land for farming

The two children walked slowly down the track. Wayra walked in front of the alpacas. Kusi walked behind. The track zigzagged from terrace to terrace. The stone terraces looked like steps in a giant staircase. Some terraces were planted in potatoes, others in corn. The terraces had been built hundreds of years ago. But many were still used today. Without them, the land would have been too steep to farm.

Soon the Urubamba River roared in the children's ears. The sun was low in the sky. The tourist buses had left for the night. Trucks full of workers were returning from work on the railway line. The boys had finished their soccer practice. All over the town, children were bringing llamas and alpacas down from the pastures. Others were returning from work in the fields.

Cooking smells filled the courtyard. Before they could eat, the children had more chores to do. Wayra fed the donkey. Kusi fed the hens and ducks and collected their eggs. The guinea pigs were her favorites. She left them until last.

"Do you have any scraps?" she asked.

"Here," said Grandmother, passing her a bowl. Kusi knew the guinea pigs were bred for food, but they were still her pets. When she counted fourteen, she knew one was in tonight's cooking pot.

Just then her mother walked in. She was wearing a beautiful shawl woven from alpaca wool. The Quechua people still used patterns from the Inca long ago. Kusi traced the pattern with her finger. She loved the bright colors. She wished she was old enough to go to the weaving school where her mother taught.

"Is Father coming home?" Wayra asked.

"How did you guess?" asked his mother.

"Grandmother always cooks guinea pig when Father comes home."

Wayra's father and brothers were porters on the Inca Way. The Inca Way was a famous trail high above the Sacred Valley. In early times, the Inca walked the trail to get to Machu Picchu.

Machu Picchu was an ancient city high in the mountains. When the Inca who lived there died, people forgot about the city. Then in 1911, Macchu Pichu was rediscovered. The jungle was cleared. The ruins were restored. Nowadays, many tourists walked the trail to visit this lost city of the Inca. It took several days to reach. People often hired porters to carry their gear.

Wayra limped outside to wait for his father and brothers. He sat beside the channel of water that ran down the middle of the street. The Inca had built **aqueducts** high in the mountains. Water flowed down the mountainside in these stone channels. When it reached the town, the townspeople used it for washing and drinking.

Wayra sat and stared at the mountains. Soon, he got an idea for a new tune. He was playing his new tune when the men arrived home.

---

aqueduct – a channel to help catch and carry water

CHAPTER TWO

Town Meeting

"I really want to go to the meeting about the new highway," Wayra said after dinner.

"It's not for children," said his father. He took off his sandals made from old car tires. He rubbed his feet.

"Why do you want to go?" asked Grandfather.

Wayra knew this was his chance to explain. But he couldn't find the right words. "It's the butterflies," he said, and everyone laughed.

"You and your butterflies," said his eldest brother, with a grin. "You live with your head in the clouds."

"What about the butterflies, Wayra?" asked Grandfather. He smiled at his grandson. "It would help if you could explain."

"It's not only the butterflies," Wayra said. "It's the birds and rare flowers as well. Once the trucks and diggers come to build this new highway, they might disappear."

One by one the family fell silent. They knew Wayra was right. Not only would the new highway destroy Inca terraces. Their rare wildlife would be threatened as well.

His father looked hard at Wayra. "Yes, son," he said. "You shall come to the meeting too."

The women gathered water from the water channel. Wayra washed with the men. Then changed into his Sunday clothes. He wore a new **crimson** poncho his mother had woven. He whistled as he walked to the town square.

Usually the villagers were watching soccer on an outdoor TV. None of Wayra's friends had their own TV. So each night families would gather in the town square to watch. But tonight the TV was switched off. People were busy putting out seats. Everyone was talking. The square buzzed with a sound like angry bees. Then the mayor arrived in his special robes.

crimson – deep red

When he banged his silver staff on the ground, everyone hushed. The mayor invited them to speak. Wayra listened carefully to what people were saying.

"I think the government should build this highway. More tourists mean more money," said one man.

"But our town is special," said another. "This new highway would destroy too many Inca ruins. After all, that's one of the things that tourists come to see."

"We need our terraces for growing food," said a man with a deep voice.

"The terraces are part of our Inca culture," said someone else.

The mayor listened to what people had to say. Then he made an announcement. "I think we should write a letter. We must remind the people of Peru about Ollantaytambo. It is the last living Inca town in the world. It's the only place on Earth where people can see how the Inca once lived. If we lose the terraces, we lose an important part of our culture."

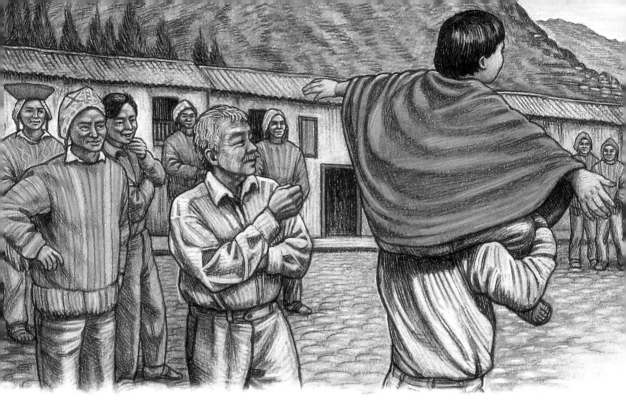

"It's not just the terraces," said a voice Wayra
knew. "My grandson has something to say."

Suddenly Wayra found himself lifted onto his
father's shoulders. He'd never spoken in front
of so many people before. When he opened his
mouth, only a squeak came out.

"Speak up," whispered Grandfather. He
reached up and held Wayra's hand.

"Don't forget all the butterflies and the
hummingbirds," Wayra said. "This valley is
famous for them as well. The trucks and diggers
might frighten them away."

The crowd rumbled their agreement. "Tell them we're happy to welcome tourists," someone said. "But the highway must go somewhere else."

It was late when the meeting finished. It was later still when the men arrived home. They sat around the cooking fire.

"You spoke well, son," said Wayra's father. He pulled a can of soda from his porter's pack. Wayra drank the sweet yellow cola with a grin on his face.

CHAPTER THREE

A Stranger Arrives

Early the next day, Wayra woke to a voice whispering in his ear. "Wake up," said Kusi. She was dressed warmly and hopping from foot to foot. "Hurry," she said. "It's Saturday."

Wayra forced his eyes open. His sister liked Saturdays because there was no school. Until now, she had been taught in Quechua. She found it easy to read and write in her own language. But this year her lessons were taught in Spanish as well. Kusi knew she would need to speak Spanish if she ever moved from her town. Yet the words sounded very strange to her ears.

"You said you'd come with me today," she reminded Wayra. "You said you'd walk all the way up the mountainside with the alpacas and me."

The sky was just getting light when the two children left. The alpacas followed in a line. They knew the route well. Kusi was happy to walk slowly. She had many questions about the meeting. But these could wait until they reached the pastures.

Wayra had a question too. He was pleased he'd spoken at the meeting. But words were not enough. There must be something else he could do. He was so busy thinking, he hardly noticed the long, slow climb.

At last they arrived at the pastures. The children left the alpacas to graze. They sat on the grass and ate their breakfast of bread and cheese. Then Kusi took out the belt she was weaving. Wayra ran his fingers along the row of golden stars. Each star sat between green zigzag mountains. "I like the pattern," he said. It was a very old pattern. Quechua women had woven it for hundreds of years.

Kusi worked with four small sticks called spindles. They had been her grandmother's spindles—and *her* grandmother's before that. Kusi threaded a different colored wool through each hole. The school where her mother taught used only ancient weaving methods. Tourists made special trips to watch the women at work. Many bought brightly colored rugs to hang on their walls back home.

Kusi looked up from her weaving. "Tell me what happened at the meeting," she said.

Wayra explained why some people wanted the new highway—but most did not.

"I think I understand," said Kusi. "It's all about tourists and the money they bring to our town. I don't like how they crowd our narrow streets and poke their heads into our courtyards. But I'm proud of living in an Inca town. This is something I want to share."

Wayra nodded. Then he lay back on the warm grass and closed his eyes. He woke as the sun reached the top of the sky. He drank from a nearby water channel. Then he played his flute. When he was troubled, making music helped him think.

"I haven't heard that tune before," said Kusi. "Is it one of your own?" Wayra nodded. "What's it about?"

"Listen and maybe you can guess." Wayra played the tune a second time.

"I think it's about the wildlife disappearing," Kusi said. "But it's sad. I don't like sad tunes."

"I like your tune," said a voice in Spanish. The two children were startled. They rarely saw strangers on this part of the mountain.

A young man stood watching them. He wore hiking boots. A large camera was slung around his neck. Wayra put down his flute and stared at the camera. When the stranger smiled, the children smiled back.

"I haven't seen a flute like this before," said the young man.

Wayra was good at his studies. He spoke
Spanish well. "It's called a *quena*," he explained.
He handed the flute to the young man. "This
one's made of bamboo. Sometimes they're
carved from llama bone."

"Very interesting," said the stranger. He
examined the flute closely, then handed it back
to Wayra. "Is there water nearby where I can fill
my bottle?"

"I'll show you," said Wayra.

Kusi watched the stranger's face as her
brother limped along the path. He showed no

surprise that Wayra was lame. They kept talking as they walked.

They were away for a long time. Kusi became worried. She was younger than her brother. But she was used to looking out for him. When she heard his flute in the distance, she relaxed. By the time she'd picked an armful of grass for the guinea pigs, he was back.

"You'll never guess," Wayra said. "Tony is making a movie about Quechua people. He wants me to be in it."

"You mean you're going to be a movie star?" Kusi said.

Wayra laughed. "It's not that kind of movie. It's a TV documentary. That's a movie that shows people real things just as they are. Tony has to speak to our parents first to ask if it's okay."

Kusi was excited for her brother. She hoped she'd be in the movie too. As they watched the alpacas, Wayra's grin stretched from ear to ear.

The children came down the mountain earlier than usual that day. Tony was arriving at seven to speak to their parents. Wayra wanted to talk to them first. This time, he walked down the mountain quicker than he ever had before. Even the alpacas seemed in a hurry to reach home.

Grandfather looked up when he heard the alpaca hoofs clacking over the stones. He was working on a new flute today. This was not a bamboo flute for selling in the market. It was a special flute carved from llama bone.

"Where's Father?" asked Wayra. He tried to keep the excitement from his voice. His father heard the question. He came out into the courtyard. By the time Wayra had finished his story, the whole family had gathered around.

"Tony's not a Spanish name," said an aunt.

"No, he's Canadian," explained Wayra. "He studied Spanish in college. He's interested in my flute. He asked all about Quechua music. I think he liked my new tune."

"Was that the tune I heard you playing before the meeting?" asked Grandfather.

"Yes." Wayra was so excited about the movie, he'd forgotten about the meeting. He'd forgotten

the very reason why his new tune was so sad.
As his family talked about Tony, Wayra began
to get an idea. But everyone was so busy asking
questions, his idea would have to wait.

"Do you think your friend would like to eat
with us?" asked Grandmother.

"Here he is," said Kusi. "Let's ask him."

Tony and the men were already talking by
the time the women carried out the food. Wayra
hoped his new friend wouldn't mind meeting so
many people. It wasn't just his immediate
family filling the courtyard. When they heard

the news, his aunts, uncles, and cousins arrived too. But what if Tony was shy?

Wayra needn't have worried. Tony was soon eating and laughing. He didn't mind at all. After Tony finished his meal, he spoke to Wayra.

"I'll begin filming tomorrow at the Pisac market," he said. "Your grandfather said you could come with him to help sell the flutes."

"Do you want me to play?" Wayra asked.

"Would you like to?"

Wayra nodded. His new tune had something important to say.

CHAPTER FOUR

Wayra's Tune

The next morning, the family got up well before the sun. After breakfast, they loaded their market goods onto an old flatbed truck. The children lay back against the soft bundles of the women's weaving. They huddled against the wool for warmth.

Kusi looked at her mother and aunts. They were wearing bright shawls and their best hats for market. Grandmother's braids were so long she could sit on them. Even though it was early, the road was full of trucks. They were all heading toward the Sunday market.

Wayra tried to sleep, but it was too noisy. The truck bumped along the road. The driver kept tooting his horn. He tooted at all his friends. He tooted at the llamas and donkeys, so they'd move out of his way. Other people did the same.

So many horns were sounding that Wayra made up a horn song inside his head.

When the family arrived at the market, they paid the driver. Everyone helped unload. "Can I carry something?" asked Tony. He had arrived with his cameras.

"It's best if we do it," the women said. They heaved great loads onto their backs.

"Is it okay if I film you?" Tony asked. Kusi hoisted a heavy load onto her back. She smiled at the camera.

Grandmother had already saved a space by the church. This was the best spot in the market. Tony sat his camera on a tripod. As the women laid out their weaving, the camera whirred.

Soon everything was ready. The women sat on the ground and began to weave. All the time they were weaving, their eyes flickered over the crowd. There was so much to see on market day. They didn't want to miss a thing.

Wayra and Grandfather took out their flutes and laid them in a row. Then Grandfather took out his llama bone flute. He began to carve.

Tony moved his tripod closer and continued to film. Wayra picked up the bamboo flute he was making. Very carefully, he carved a new hole. From time to time he looked up at the camera. He hoped Tony wouldn't forget to ask him to play his new tune. He not only wanted to play it. He also wanted to tell people what it was about. He wanted to tell them why the new highway should not be built. But would he be brave enough when the time came?

More and more buses arrived. More and more tourists filled the market. They gathered around the church. Many stopped to admire the weaving and flutes. Grandmother bargained with them and made a lot of sales. The money would buy meat and maybe a chicken too. It would buy hot chili peppers and some fruit. The rest of the money would pay for clothing and school fees.

After a time, Tony went off to film the rest of the market. "Here," said Grandmother. She gave Wayra and Kusi a few coins to spend.

The two children looked around the market together. Kusi admired the jewelry. Wayra stopped in front of a stall of soccer uniforms. He was looking at a red jersey when he heard Tony call. "Wayra, it's time for you to play."

When Wayra picked up his flute, Grandfather stopped him. "It's not every day you get to play in a movie," he said. He put the new llama bone flute into his grandson's hands.

"Oh," said Wayra, although he really meant "thank you." Grandfather could tell from his face that he was pleased.

"Let's find a quiet place," said Tony. "Isn't the river near here?"

Tony was weighted down with his camera and tripod. He was happy to walk slowly, and Wayra had no trouble keeping up. Soon they left the market and were standing beside the river.

The Urubamba flowed more quietly than in Ollantaytambo. "I must practice first," Wayra said. "It's a new flute. I need to hear its voice." Before he began, he looked closely at the carvings. Grandfather had carved all the wild creatures Wayra loved best. There was a giant condor. A hummingbird was whirring its wings. A butterfly sat on a mountain flower.

Tony began filming as Wayra played. Some tunes he recognized. Others he had not heard before. Wayra played his new tune last. He became so lost in the music that he forgot about the camera. When he finished, he put his flute down and looked up at the mountains.

Tony spoke into the camera. "The last tune was composed by this young Quechua boy. Wayra, can you tell us what your tune is about?"

The mountains gave Wayra courage. This was his chance to tell people his message. He coughed and lifted his head. As he started to speak, Tony let the camera run.

"My song is about the wild creatures that live on the mountains near my home," said Wayra. Tony nodded. "I live in Ollantaytambo. It is the only living Inca town in the world. The Inca

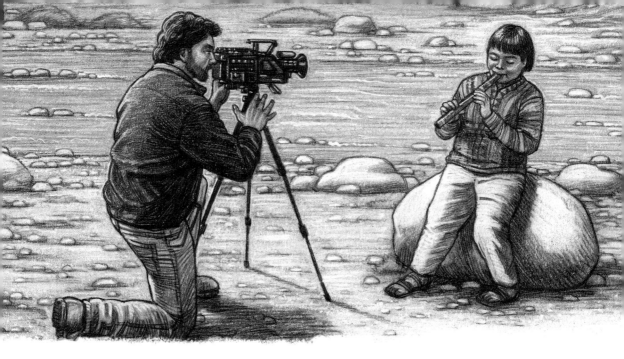

were my ancestors. Over five hundred years ago they built wonderful stone terraces. We still use some of them for farming today."

As Wayra spoke he could see everything clearly in his mind.

"The Inca also built a mighty fortress and temple in Ollantaytambo. They were clever builders. A lot of their stonework still stands today. Now there are plans to build a new highway. People say it will bring more tourists to the Sacred Valley. But if the highway goes ahead, a hundred Inca terraces will be destroyed. It's not only the terraces. There are over a hundred native butterflies near where

I live. There are fifteen different kinds of hummingbirds. There are giant condors with wing spans ten feet wide."

Wayra looked at Tony, who nodded and smiled. "My sister says my new tune is sad," continued Wayra. "She's right. It's sad because if the new highway is built, the terraces and wildlife might disappear. Maybe my tune can help save them." Wayra stopped speaking, but didn't move. He stared into the camera lens until Tony stopped filming.

Tony packed away the tripod. Wayra looked thoughtfully at the movie camera as Tony polished the lens. "Thank you," Tony said. "You did well. I'll send you a video of my film. Maybe your friends would like to watch it on the TV in the town square."

"I don't think so," said Wayra. "My friends are more interested in soccer than in watching me play the flute."

"You never know," said Tony. "But the important thing is your message will reach people around the world."

CHAPTER FIVE

A Song of Thanks

The next few months passed slowly. Some days it seemed to Wayra that the filming had never happened. Each time he played his new tune, he thought about its message.

No machines had arrived yet to build the new highway. The blue butterfly with the pink splash on its wing was still there. Maybe the mayor's letter or the documentary had helped after all. Or maybe the road builders were already on their way. Then one night Wayra and Kusi returned from the mountain with the alpacas. A special visitor was waiting.

"Hi," said Tony. He gave them a big grin. While Grandmother led the alpacas away, Wayra and Kusi began asking questions.

Tony laughed. "Slow down," he said. "I have something for you."

He opened his backpack and took out a box. He placed the box in Wayra's hands. Inside was a video. On its cover was a photograph of Wayra playing his flute.

"Everyone likes it," Tony said. "They especially like your tune."

Wayra passed the video to Grandmother and Grandfather. They passed it to Kusi. "How many people have seen it?" Kusi asked.

"We translated the documentary into several languages," explained Tony. "Soon many thousands of people will watch it on TV."

Wayra said nothing for a long time. He sat quietly while Grandmother passed food around and poured cups of tea. He was thinking about how movies were able to carry messages around the world. He was thinking that his world, which had always seemed so big, suddenly seemed small.

"That's good news," Wayra said. "I hope many people will listen to my message." He smiled at his new friend. "I have a gift for you as well," he said. "I've been working on a new tune."

"I hope this one is a happy one," said Kusi.

Wayra took out his flute and played his new tune. Kusi's feet danced. The notes skipped up and down. "It's a thank-you song," Wayra said when he finished playing. "It's to thank you for carrying my message to so many people around the world."

Tony looked pleased.

"I won't play it again until the government agrees to build the highway someplace else," said Wayra. "I'll play it when I know that our terraces are safe and the wildlife has been saved."

"Then I'll come back and make another movie," said Tony.

Wayra looked at the camera hanging around Tony's neck. "Maybe you can teach me how to make movies," he said. "Maybe one day I can be a movie maker like you."

Everyone laughed, except Grandfather. He smiled at Wayra. Then he picked up his flute and played the tune of the condor. As Wayra listened, he imagined he was the giant bird. He was flying from mountaintop to mountaintop, looking down on the world.

Quechua Culture

The story you just read is fictional. That means it was made up. But many things about the story are true. Some people in Peru still live as the Inca did. Quechua music is played as it has been for centuries. And tourism really is important.

Inca Culture

Peru was once home to the Inca Empire. Reminders of the Inca still stand today. People visit Inca ruins such as Machu Picchu. Villagers still rely on ancient aqueducts to channel water. People also grow crops along the terraces that the Inca carved.

Quechua Music

The Quechua people still play ancient Inca songs. They use traditional instruments such as the *quena*. This is a flute carved from bamboo or llama bone. The songs tell stories about the animals, land, and people of Peru.

Tourism in the Andes

Tourism brings money into Peru. It also allows Peru to share its culture. But careless visitors can damage Inca ruins. The ruins at Machu Picchu may be crumbling because of too many visitors. Today, people are trying to create tourism that does not harm the land.

Create a Travel Brochure

You read about the town of Ollantaytambo in Peru. Now help people learn more about Peru. Create a brochure that tells people what they can see and do on their travels.

- Research at the library or online. Find out about festivals, food, and fun things to do.

- Decide what to show in your brochure. What is special about Peru?

- Give each column a heading, such as "For Kids" or "What to See." Write a paragraph for each.

- Search for pictures of Peru, or draw your own.

- Put your text and pictures together to make a brochure. Use the model below as an example.

For Kids	Festivals	What to See

47

Read More About Other Cultures

Find and read more books about countries in South America. As you read, think about these questions. They will help you understand more about other cultures.

- What is life like in this country?

- What is special about this country?

- How is this country changing?

- What are people doing to keep their traditions alive?

SUGGESTED READING
Reading Expeditions
Communities Around the World:
Caracas, Venezuela